PIXNEXUS

COMPANION HANDBOOK

2nd Edition

BOOK DESIGN	Isabella La Rocca
ISBN-10	1478355530
ISNB-13	978-1478355533

Contents

The Meaning of Everything: RESOLUTION

We are in the midst of a revolution. In the last quarter century, the tools used to create imagery have evolved into a new form: digital media. Digital media is infinitely reproducible, it's much more editable, and it's usually more convenient than analog media. But arguably, digital imagery is just a simulation and synthesis of analog media that has existed for hundreds or thousands of years, such as drawing, painting, photography, and motion pictures. Now all of these are created and/or manipulated digitally.

But there is an inarguable and essential difference between the analog universe, in which we live and breathe, and the digital universe. To the best of our knowledge, the analog universe is not made up of a single, discrete element. In fact, the smaller things are, the more complex they are.

The digital universe, however, is made of discrete elements. All digital media can all be boiled down to long strings of one discrete element: the bit. The word bit is short for "<u>bi</u>nary dig<u>it</u>." A bit has only two possibilities - 1 or 0, on or off, yes or no, true or false, white or black; the same amount of information as a basic light switch.

So the digital universe is made up of discrete steps, like a staircase. And the analog universe is like a ramp – it's continuous. If you have many steps very close together, they become relatively so small that the staircase simulates a ramp.

With the possible exception of vector-based files,* digital images are made up of discrete elements called pixels, short for "picture elements." Every digital photograph, every frame of a motion picture, every Photoshop file is nothing but a grid of pixels, also referred to as a raster or sometimes a bitmap. If you have enough pixels very close together they become so small that you get the illusion of a continuous tone image.

---

* Vector-based files: see *Chapter 5*.

For a digital image to achieve the illusion of a continuous tone image, it must have enough resolution, that is, enough pixels so that you are not aware of the pixels and all you see is a continuous tone image.

There are three practical ways of expressing image resolution:

1. Image resolution is most accurately expressed as **pixel dimensions**, not as DPI.*. The pixel dimensions of an image are defined as the number of pixels horizontally, or width, by the number of pixels vertically, or height.

2. When working with digital cameras, resolution is often expressed in **megapixels (MP)**. One megapixel equals about a million pixels. You can calcuate the number of pixels in an image by multiplying the width in pixels by the height in pixels.

3. If you intend to make a print from your file, you also need to know the number of pixels per inch, also known as **PPI,** which will make a continuous tone image. You need between 240 and 400 ppi, depending on the paper and the printer.

If you only know the maximum resolution of a camera in megapixels, you won't know the exact pixel dimensions nor the exact size of the print - check the camera menu or manual for the pixel dimensions of the file. To calculate the size of your print at optical resolution,** divide the pixel dimensions by the number of pixels per inch. The following table includes most of the standard image sizes.

* DPI or dots per inch is sometimes used to refer to the number of samples of light a scanner takes in each inch, the number of dots of light a computer monitor displays, or the number of dots of ink an inkjet printer sprays. See *Chapter 4.*

** Optical resolution is from the original source, that is, from the light. Practically, interpolation is enlarging a smaller grid of pixels into a larger grid of pixels. See *Chapter 4.*

Image Resolution and Equivalent Print Sizes Without Interpolation

MP	pixel dimensions	print size @ 240PPI in inches	print size @ 300PPI in inches	print size @ 400PPI in inches
.3	640 X 480	2.67 X 2	2.13 X 1.6	1.6 X 1.2
1.2	1280 X 960	5.3 X 4	4.25 X 3.2	3.2 X 2.4
2	1600 X 1200	16.7 X 5	5.33 X 4	4 X 3
2	1920 X 1080	8 X 4.5	6.4 X 3.6	4.8 X 2.7
2.2	1800 X 1200	7.5 X 5	6 X 4	4.5 X 3
3	2048 X 1536	8.53 X 6.4	6.82 X 5.12	5.12 X 4.09
3.1	2100 X 1500	8.75 X 6.25	7 X 5	5.25 X 3.75
3.9	2272 X 1704	9.47 X 7.1	7.57 X 5.68	5.68 X 4.26
4	2464 X 1632	10.27 X 6.8	8.21 X 5.44	6.16 X 4.08
4.9	2560 X 1920	10.67 X 8	8.53 X 6.4	6.4 X 4.8
6	3008 X 2000	12.53 X 8.33	10.2 X 6.7	7.52 X 5
6.3	3072 X 2048	12.8 X 8.53	10 X 6.8	7.68 X 5.12
10	3648 X 2736	15.2 X 11.4	12.16 X 9.12	9.12 X 6.84
11	4064 X 2704	16.93 X 11.27	13.5 X 9	10.16 X 6.76
12	4290 X 2800	17.883 X 11.7	14.30 X 9.34	10.73 X 7
12.1	4000 X 3000	16.67 X 12.5	13.33 X 10	10 X 7.5
12.2	4272 X 2848	17.8 X 11.9	14.24 X 16.16	10.68 X 7.12
14.1	4320 X 3240	18 X 13.5	14.4 X 10.8	10.8 X 8.1
14.3	4352 X 3264	18.13 X 13.6	14.5 X 10.88	10.8 X 8.1
14.7	4416 X 3312	18.4 X 13.8	14.72 X 11.04	11.04 X 8.28
15.1	4752 X 3168	19.8 X 13.2	15.84 X 10.56	11.88 X 7.92
16	4608 X 3456	19.2 X 14.4	15.36 X 11.52	11.52 X 8.64
16.1	4896 X 3264	20.4 X 13.6	16.32 X 10.85	12.24 X 8.16
16.2	4928 X 3280	20.53 X 13.67	16.43 X 10.93	12.32 X 8.2
18	5184 X 3456	21.6 X 14.4	17.28 X 11.52	12.96 X 8.64
21	5616 X 3744	23.4 X 15.6	18.72 X 12.48	14.04 X 9.36
22.3	5760 X 3840	24 X 16	19.2 X 12.8	14.4 X 9.6
24.2	6016 X 4000	25.07 X 16.67	20.05 X 13.33	15.04 X 10
24.5	6048 X 4032	25.2 X 16.8	20.06 X 13.44	15.12 X 10.08
36.3	7360 X 4912	30.67 X 20.47	24.53 X 16.37	18.4 X 12.28
37.5	7500 X 5000	31.25 X 20.8	25 X 16.67	18.75 X 12.5

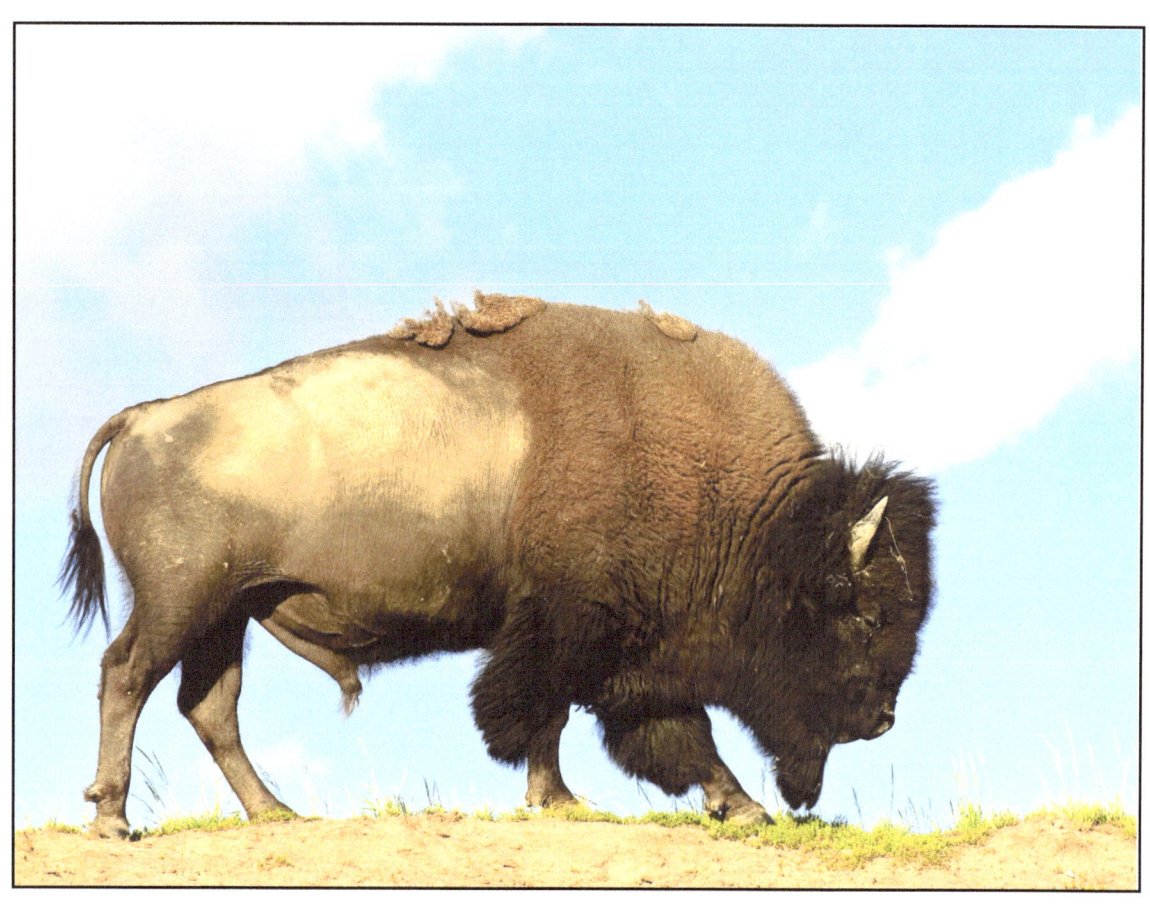

Let's take for example, this 10MP 3,648 pixel by 2,736 pixel image.

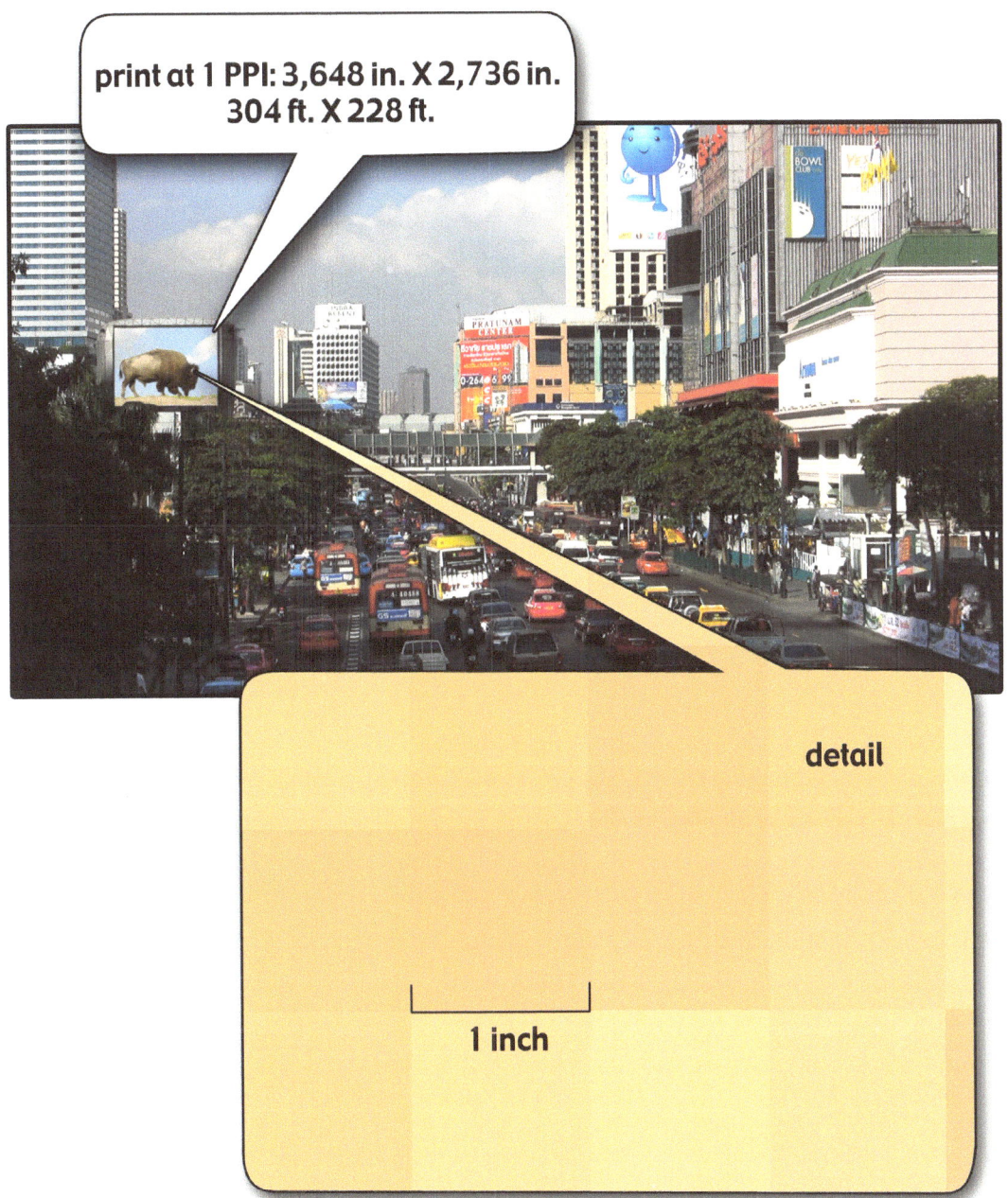

At 1 PPI, it would make a giant, super-pixelated print - pixels that are one inch square.

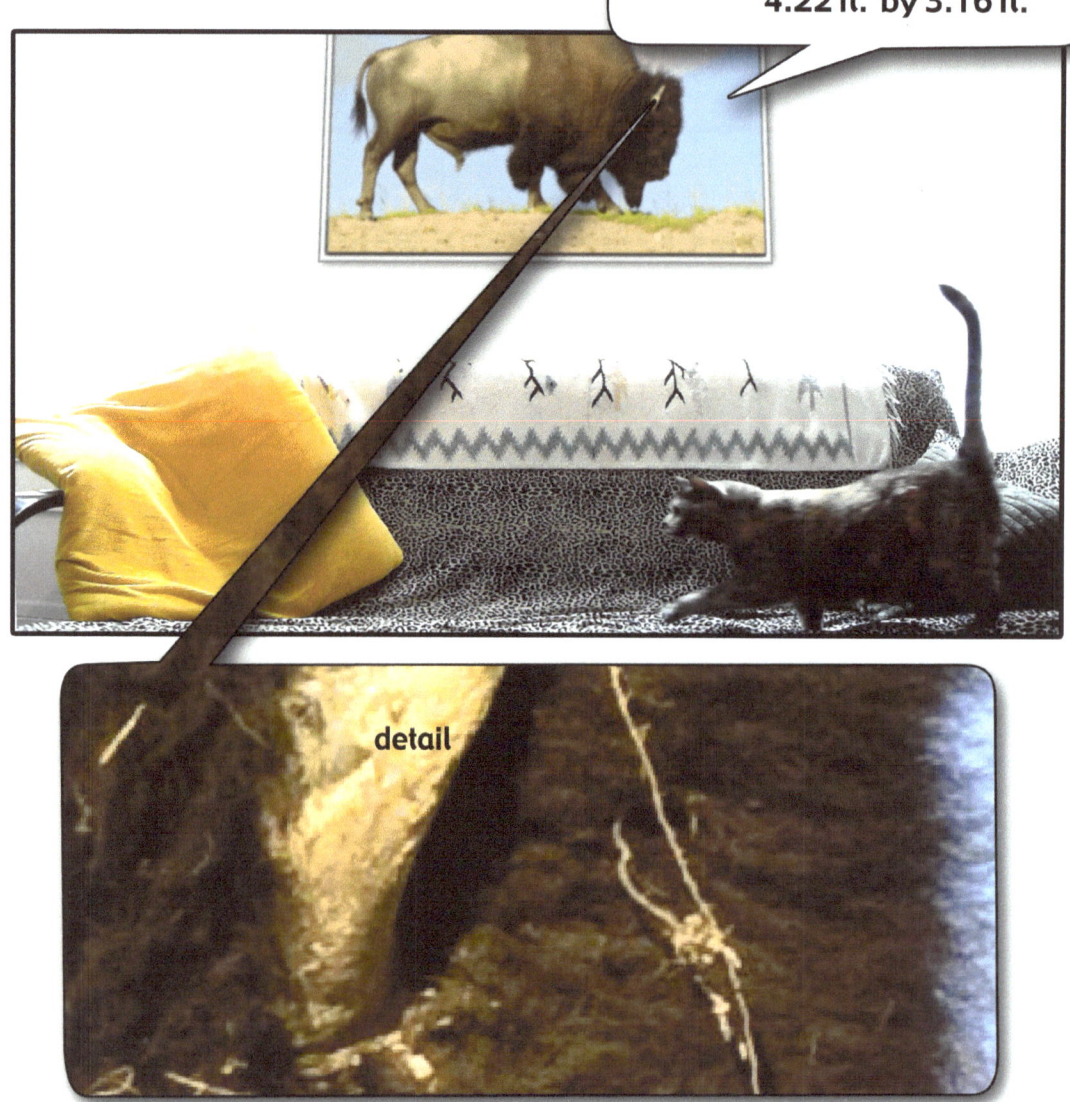

print at 72 PPI: 50.67 in. X 38 in.
4.22 ft. by 3.16 ft.

detail

At 72 PPI, it would make a large (3,648 px X 2,736 px ÷ 72) but pixelated print.

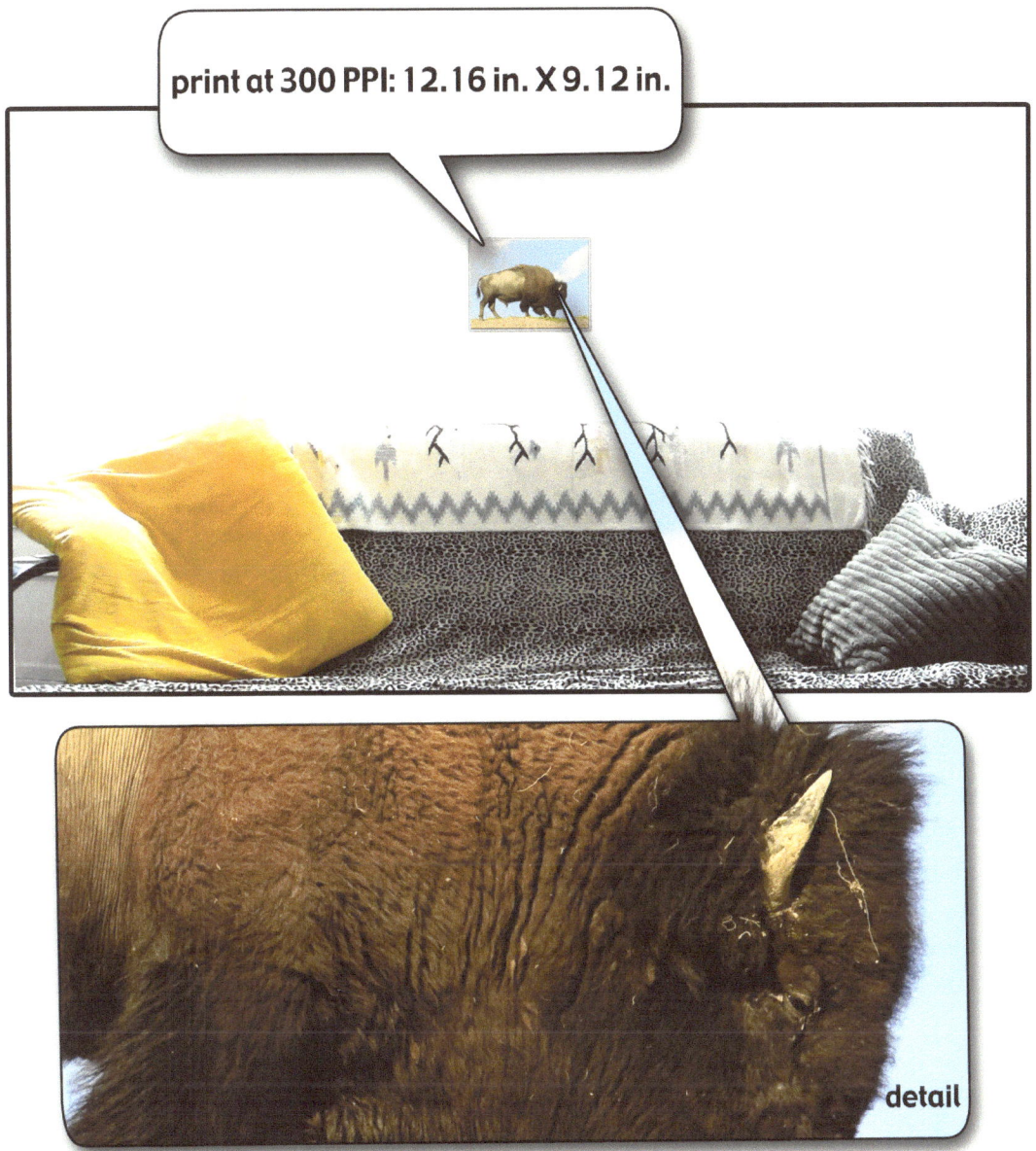

print at 300 PPI: 12.16 in. X 9.12 in.

detail

At 300 PPI, it would make a smaller (3,648 px X 2,736 px ÷ 300) print that has enough pixels in each inch that you are no longer aware of the pixels and all you see is the continuous tone image. If you need a larger print from the file, you'll need to interpolate (also called resample)*.

* Optical resolution is from the original source, that is, from the light. Practically, interpolation means enlarging a smaller grid of pixels into a larger grid of pixels. See the *Chapter 4*.

PLAY NICE: WORKFLOW

1. Pixel Capture or Pixel Creation

Many pixels originate from light. These pixels are captured with a digital camera or a scanner. Or you may create pixels digitally using a software application, many of which are listed in the graph on the following page.

Pixels must be encoded in a file. There are a variety of file formats, which can be encoded and read by different software applications and which are identified by a 3-or-4-letter extension. File formats can be divided into uncompressed file formats and compression file formats. Compression formats can be divided into lossless codecs (short for **co**mpression/**dec**ompression) and lossy codecs. Lossless compression ensures that even though the file size is reduced when the file is closed, all of the original data is recovered when the file is opened. Lossy compression reduces the file size by permanently discarding information, though hopefully not information that compromises the integrity of the image. There are many kinds of raw files, which are uncompressed, unprocessed digital camera files that give you the ultimate control over your images.

It's sometimes possible to output directly to screen or print, but usually the next step is to manage your files.

2. File Management

File management applications let you preview, discard, organize, rename, and even assign ratings, keywords, and other metadata to your files, without having to open each file. They also have advanced search functions, which make it easier to find the file in the future. They save time, especially if you're working with files from a digital camera.

At the very least, you'll use your operating system to discard, organize, and rename your files. Then it's not unlikely that you'll want to manipulate and composite your image in a software application, many of which are listed in the following illustrations.

pixel capture

digital camera   **scanner**

raw   .tiff

.tiff   .jpeg

.jpeg

pixel creation

Adobe Photoshop .psd

Adobe Illustrator .ai

Corel Painter .rif

Adobe Flash .fla

CAD applications

3-D applications

mobile apps

file management

Adobe Lightroom

Apple Aperture

Adobe Bridge

3. Single-Layer Batch Processing and/or Multi-Layer Compositing

Notice that most file management applications are also, or also give you access to, single-layer batch processing (Camera Raw can be opened through Adobe Bridge). This is most useful for digital photos. These applications allow you to make adjustments to your images, such as color correction, tonal adjustments, sharpening, noise removal, and retouching. Most of these adjustments are global rather than local, that is, they affect the whole image not just a specific area of the image. They also make it easy to apply any of the adjustments to multiple images (batch processing).

If you want to make local adjustments, or if you want to composite several images along with text, styles, or filters, the go-to application is Adobe Photoshop. Photoshop can open or import files from many applications, including all the pixel creation applications. Photoshop has thrived for so long because of its use of layers. There are also other multi-layer processing applications, such as GIMP, which is open-source and free, though arguably not as extensive or user-friendly as Photoshop.

It's easy to maintain fluidity between single-layer batch processing applications and Photoshop (see left arrow in the illustration on the next page).* If you intend to work with Photoshop, it's best to make a master file at the original resolution in the original color profile,** which contains all your smart objects, layers, masks, styles, and filters. Your Photoshop master file should always be in .psd format, because that's Photoshop's native file format. The master file is the one you guard with your life, or at least back up regularly.

*   After processing an image in Camera Raw always open the file in Photoshop as a smart object by shift-clicking on the Open Image button, which changes it to Open Object (see right arrow in the illustration on the next page). Then you can at anytime tweak your Camera Raw adjustments in your master file by opening (double-clicking on) the smart object.

**   For more about color profiles see *Chapter 6.*

single-layer batch processing

Adobe Lightroom

Apple Aperture

Camera Raw (Bridge)

multi-layer compositing: Photoshop

master.psd @ original resolution and color space

smart objects

layers

masks

styles

filters

4. Output: Screen or Print

There are many ways to output your image or to integrate your image into your final product: a print project such as a book or brochure; a web site; a film, animation, or video; a disc. Most of these applications read .psd files, but depending on how you will use the file, you may need to make a copy of the file in a different format.

Note that you can also often print or export for screen from pixel creation applications, listed on page 9.

You can usually print to your desktop printer directly from your .psd master file, though if it's a large file with lots of layers and smart objects, etc. it may be best to print from a copy that's been flattened.

If you're having your image printed elsewhere, you'll need to check with the print service as to the proper file format. You may also need to change the color profile* of the copy of your master file so it's the same color profile as the printer. If you need to enlarge the image, do not resample (also called interpolation)** your master file – it's always best to keep your precious original pixels unchanged; always resample a copy of the file. Usually, your print service will ask for a .tiff or a .pdf.   If they ask for a .jpg, make sure you give them a .jpg at maximum quality so as not to lose image-quality in the compression.

If you intend to post your image on the Internet, the application used to read the file is a web browser (Google Chrome, Mozilla Firefox, Safari, Internet Explorer, and Opera are the most popular). All web browsers read .jpg and .gif formats, but all the latest browsers also read .png format.

If you're e-mailing your image, unless your recipient has the specific application you're working with, it's best to e-mail the file in a format that a web browser reads, so your recipient can see the image.

---

*   For more about color management and color profiles, see **Chapter 6**.

**   For more about interpolation, see **Chapter 4**.

print

.psd
.tiff
.pdf

page layout

Adobe InDesign

Microsoft Word

Quark XPress

motion

Avid

Apple Final Cut

Adobe Premiere

Apple Photoshop

Apple After Effects

3-d animation applications

web

.jpeg
.gif
.png

web authoring

Adobe Dreamweaver

disc

Apple DVD Studio Pro

Apple Encore

Sea of Possibilities: BITS AND BYTES

What is a bit?

Short for "<u>bi</u>nary dig<u>it</u>," a bit can be thought of as an electrical switch or a toggle. It's 2 possibilities: 1 or 0, on or off, yes or no, true or false, white or black. Each of those possibilities can lead to 2 more possibilities; that's 2 times 2 possibilities or a total of 4 possibilities. Each of those possibilities can lead to 2 more possibilities and each of those possibilities can lead to 2 more possibilities and so on and on and on and on. Any number can be generated using this binary system, which results in vast amounts of information.

$$2 \times 2 = 4; \quad 4 \times 2 = 8; \quad 8 \times 2 = 16...$$

A byte is 8 bits or 2^8 or 256 possibilities. This is about the amount of information necessary to generate one letter of the alphabet in a text file. For example, binary code for the letter "Z" is 01011010.

The following table lists practical examples of the quantities of information necessary to generate or store data, and will help demystify file size and disc storage size.

Units of Information and Examples		
UNIT	**EQUIVALENT**	**EXAMPLES**
byte	8 bits	one text character
kilobyte (KB)	1024 (2^{10}) bytes	one-page word processing file ≈ 30 KB website homepage < 100 KB
megabyte (MB)	1024 kilobytes	one frame uncompressed video ≈ 6 MB hard drive 1983 computer = 10 MB 8" X 10" RGB print res .psd > 13 MB 20" X 30" RGB print res .psd > 154 MB data Compact Disc (CD) = 700 MB
gigabyte (GB)	1024 megabytes	single-layer DVD = 4.7 GB single-layer Blu-ray disc = 25 GB flash drive = 256 MB - 64 GB
terabyte (TB)	1024 gigabytes	hard drive 2014 computer = 500 GB - 3 TB
petabyte (PB)	1024 terabytes	Google processes over 20 PB of data per day
exabyte (EB)	1024 petabytes	all the printed material in the world ≈ 5 EB
zettabyte (ZB)	1024 exabytes	250 billion DVDs ≈ 1 ZB

How many bits are necessary to make a pixel?

An image pixel is a rectangle of color; a screen pixel is a dot of color. Either way, the greater the bit depth, the more colors are possible for each pixel to display. Understanding bit depth is fundamental to understanding color in digital media.

Bit depth is easiest to understand by comparing 1-bit images to images with greater bit-depth. One bit is the equivalent of 2 possibilities, so each pixel in a 1-bit color image can only display only 1 of 2 colors.

Early personal computer monitors were 1-bit color monitors, so they only displayed 2 colors. Some monitors displayed black and white, others black and amber, and others black and green.

Things improved a lot when 8-bit monitors (256 colors) came along. These days 256 colors can also be used to refer to gray-scale images (256 levels of gray from black to white).

Current computer monitors display 24-bit color, also referred to as 16.7 million colors (2^{24} = 16,777,216). That may seem like a lot of colors, but it's still not as large or nuanced as the color space that you perceive with your eyes.*

Don't confuse bit-depth with resolution. Bit depth is the number of bits to each pixel, resolution is the number of pixels in each image.

It's important to remember that the bit-depth of an image may be different than the bit-depth of the monitor. For example, a 24-bit color image displayed on a 1-bit monitor will only appear in 2 colors, a1-bit image displayed on a state of the art 24-bit monitor, will still only be black and white, and a 48-bit color image displayed on a 24-bit monitor will only appear in 24-bit color.**

---

* For more about color space, see the *Chapter 6*.

** For more about resolution, see *Chapter 1* and *Chapter 4*.

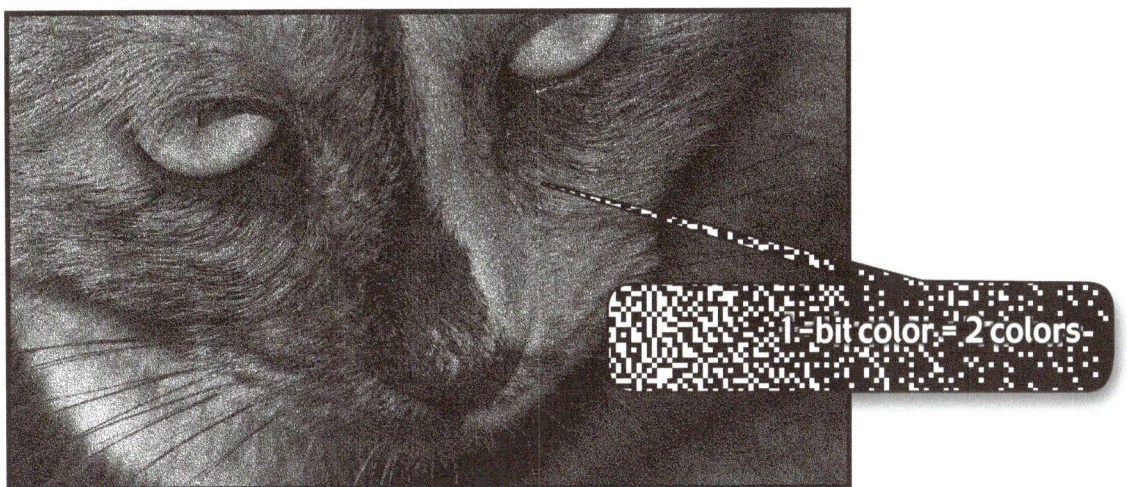

1-bit color = 2 colors

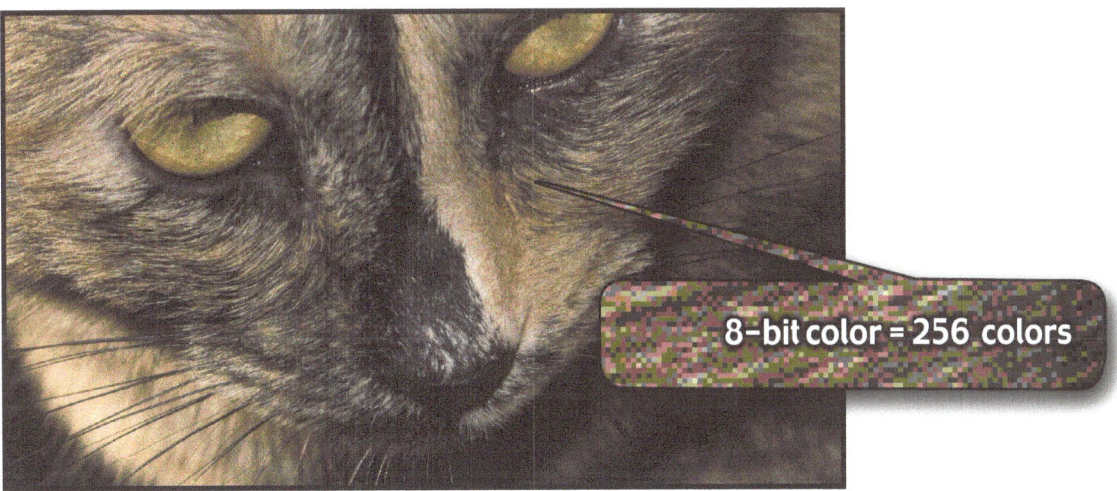

8-bit color = 256 colors

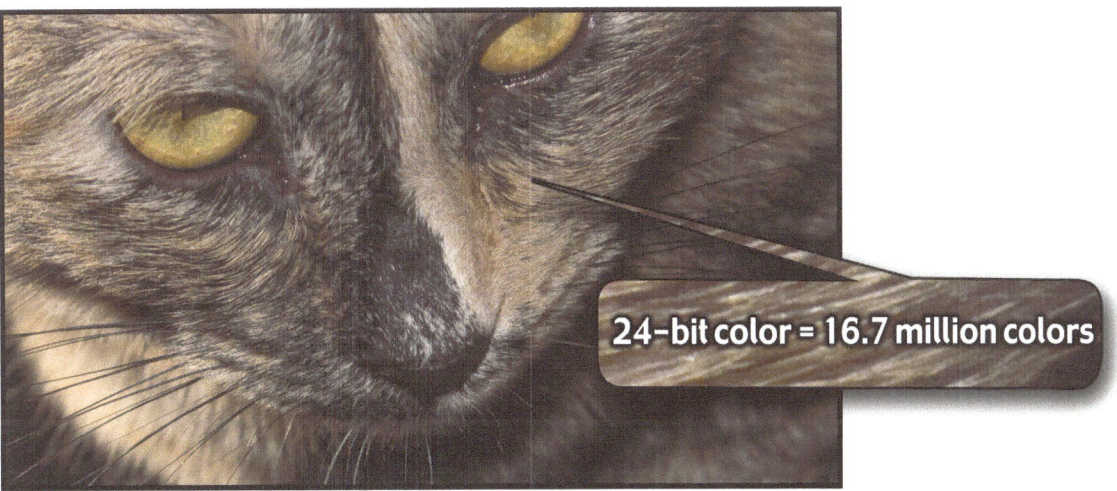

24-bit color = 16.7 million colors

RESOLUTION REDUX: **DOTS AND SQUARES**

Pixels Per Inch (PPI) versus Dots Per Inch (DPI)

PPI is a way of expressing image resolution, specifically for print.* The pixels that make up image files are always square except for certain kinds of video files, which are rectangular.

The term DPI is sometimes used to express screen resolution, like that of computer monitors and projectors. It is also used to indicate the resolution of an ink jet printer. And it can be used to determine the resolution of a scan.

1. Screen Resolution

A computer monitor is a light box that allows you to view digital imagery and text using an array of dots of light, also known as screen pixels.

The early personal Macintosh computer monitors displayed 514 dots of light horizontally by 384 dots of light vertically on a 9 inch screen - 9" is the measurement of the screen on the diagonal. The actual viewable screen size was approximately 7.14" X 5.33." This is the origin of the now almost meaningless screen resolution setting of 72DPI – there were approximately 72 dots of light in each linear inch of a 7.14" X 5.33" computer monitor with a screen resolution of 514 X 384. But no one is using these low-res monitors anymore!

---

* For more about image resolution, see **_Chapter 1_**.

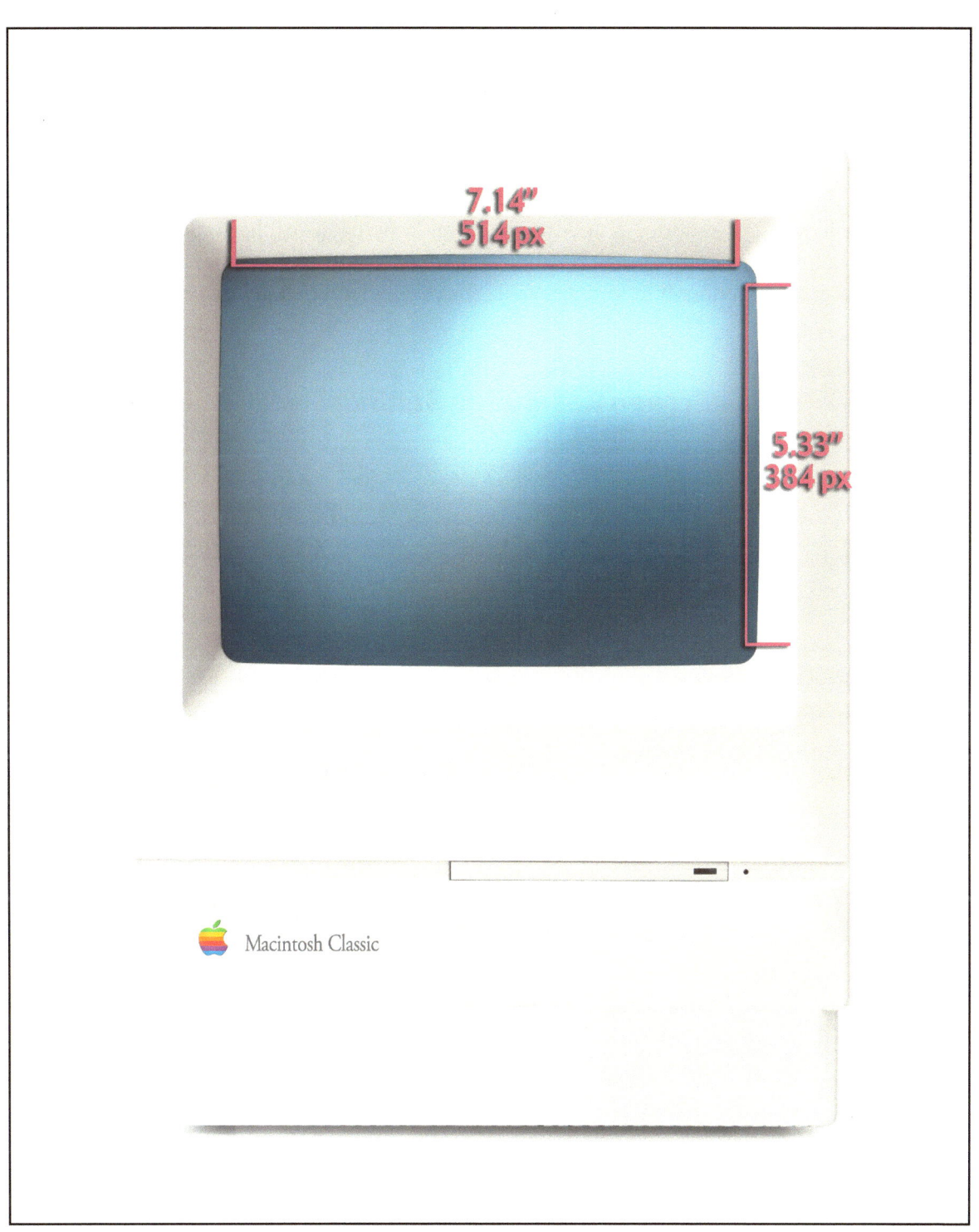

7.14"
514 px

5.33"
384 px

Macintosh Classic

1. Screen Resolution continued

These days laptops and computer monitors allow you to choose your resolution settings. Mobile displays such as tablets and smart phones have the advantage that they can be oriented horizontally or vertically. When preparing images for the screen, DPI is not a useful way of expressing resolution. Knowing the pixel dimensions of the screen is much more useful. Screen resolution increases with each new version but it's easy enough to find it for whichever device you may be using.

Screen Resolution Settings	
27" LED flat screen settings	800 X 600 1024 X 768 1280 X 720 1280 X 720 1280 X 1024 1344 X 756 1600 X 900 1600 X 1200 1680 X 1050 1920 X 1080 1920 X 1200 2560 X 1440
Apple iPad Air	2048 X 1536
Google Nexus 7	1920 X 1200
Amazon Kindle Fire HDX	2560 X 1600
Samsung Galaxy s5	1920 X 1080
Apple iPhone 5S and iPod touch	1136 X 640

2. Printer Resolution

You may also encounter the term DPI in relation to printer resolution. Inkjet printers spray tiny dots of ink onto paper to create a print. DPI refers to the number of dots of ink in each linear inch of the print. For example, a state-of-the-art desktop photo inkjet printer has a resolution of 4800 by 2400 DPI. That means it sprays 4,800 dots of ink an inch across and 2,400 rows of ink an inch down. This is plenty of ink to make a rich, glorious print *if* you have enough image resolution. But if you were print say, a 1PPI file, you'd have printed a beautifully rendered, low resolution image.

3. Scanner Resolution

Scanners also define resolution in terms of DPI, which is a misnomer; it would be more accurate to define scanner resolution as samples per inch.

Scanners sample the light reflected from a print, or transmitted through a negative or transparency. Ideally, one sample of light becomes one pixel - a square of color, which closely approximates the color of the original sample. One way of defining optical resolution is: one sample of light equals one pixel. But scanners are also able to interpolate by using one sample of light to create more than one pixel. Interpolation algorithms use the information of the surrounding pixels to guess the colors of the made up pixels. Most scanners are able to scan with enough optical resolution that the only reason you'd want to interpolate is if you want to make a print that's much larger than your original. Photoshop's interpolation algorithms are usually better than those of scanner software.

In any case, your master file should always be kept at the original, optical resolution. You can always make a copy that you interpolate for enlargement. The best pixels are pixels from the light.

Pixels and Paths: **RASTER AND VECTOR**

A raster image is formed by a grid of pixels. The more pixels in the grid, the higher the resolution. A vector image is resolution independent.

We'll use the Cartesian co-ordinate system and a simple graphic to better understand why this is true. The x-axis represents the horizontal value and the y-axis represents the vertical value. The point that represents the right eye can be defined by the numerals 3 for the x value and 3 for the y value. The left eye can be defined by the numerals -3 and 3. The smile can be represented by similar values, to indicate the vector or path between the two points that define it, with just a little more information to specify the curve, which isn't necessary to explain here.

Because these are vectors, we can blow this up as big as we want without losing quality - it's resolution independent.

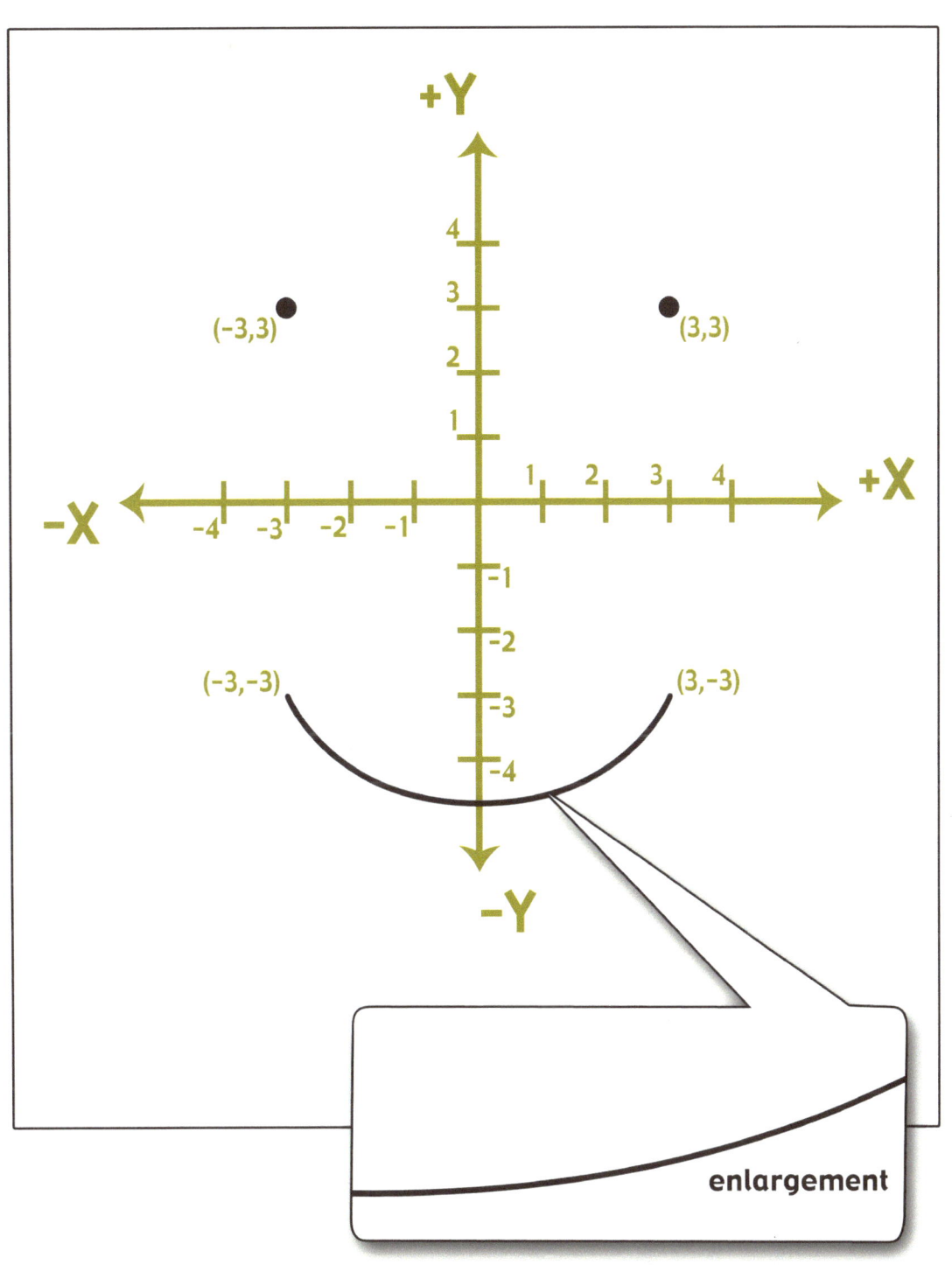

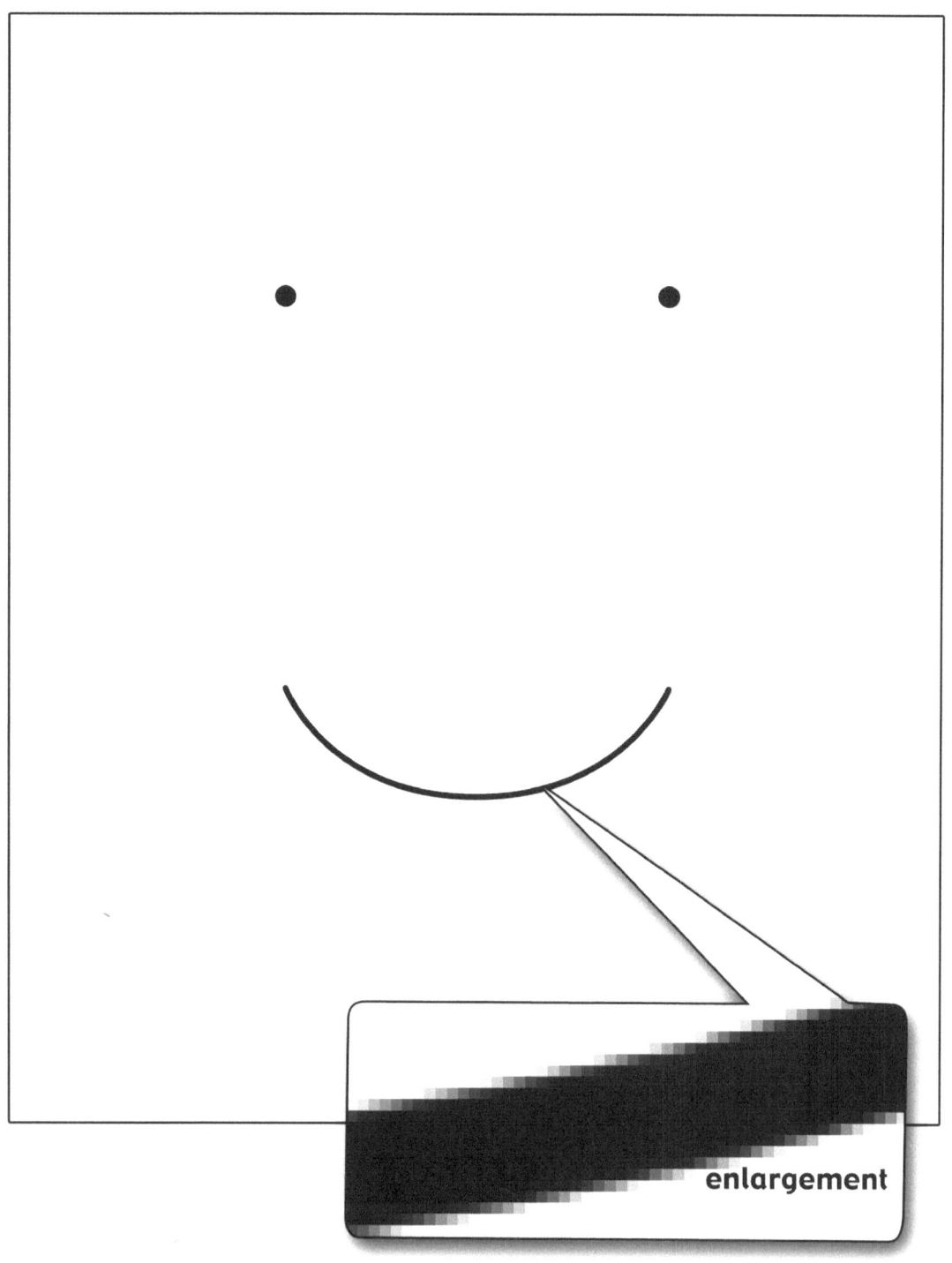

enlargement

The 1-bit depth* raster version of this simple graphic requires 1,913 X 1,642 pixels, which results in a much bigger file than the vector graphic. If we enlarge the raster graphic, we lose resolution (smoothness and clarity).

Vector formats are best for graphics with large flat areas of color and simple gradients, like logos, maps, or fonts. But they're not so great for continuous tone images, like photographs. Even a homogenous sky in a photograph is made up of many shades of blue. A cloud is even more nuanced. It's not unusual to rasterize a vector graphic so that you can work with it in a bitmap application. But it can be tricky to work with a raster image in a vector application.

Illustrator and Flash are the most commonly used vector graphics software applications. Computer-Aided Design applications can generate both vector and bitmap files. Photoshop and Painter are bitmap applications. Photoshop also has features that function much like those of a vector application, for example, the pen tool, paths, vector masks, shape layers, gradient fill layers, and solid color fill layers.**

* For more about bit depth, see *Chapter 3*.

** For more about software applications, see *Chapter 2*.

COLOR

———

Imagine you're a kind of sea creature, like a sea anemone, deep down at the botom of the ocean. And all around you waves are forming in reaction to what's going on in the water... Now imagine the feeling of those waves all around you. Imagine that from the feeling of the waves against your body, you can tell all sorts of things about sea around you. You know where the fish around you are and how big they are and the directions they're moving. You know where the coral and the kelp is and where the other sea creatures are, and how big they are and where they're going - all from the feeling of the waves against your body.

In fact, that's what your eyes are doing right now. Just from waves reflected from or transmitted through the objects around you, you can tell all sorts of things about your world. Light is the waves that our eyes perceive. And color is light and our perception of it. Color has been studied by artists and scientists for centuries and we're still learning about it!

We are surrounded by all kinds of waves, quantified as the electromagnetic spectrum (see illustration on right). Different media and devices such as radios, microwaves, infrared film, and x-rays make use of specific wavelengths, but we can't see those waves directly. We can only see less than 1% of the electromagnetic spectrum. That less than 1% is called the human visible light spectrum. So one way of describing color is in terms of its frequency or its wavelength on the electromagnetic spectrum.The color red has the longest waves and violet has the shortest waves. In between are all the colors of the rainbow.

Ultraviolet waves are invisible to humans. But flies are able to see ultraviolet light. In fact, spiders weave floral patterns that reflect ultraviolet light into their webs to attract prey. So we can say that a fly's **color space** is different than ours.

Our perception of color is relative - it changes according to the surrounding colors and even our individual backgrounds and biases. Different digital devices and media (scanners, monitors, printers) also have different color spaces. Our challenge is to maintain the intended colors of our images throughout the process.

the electromagnetic spectrum

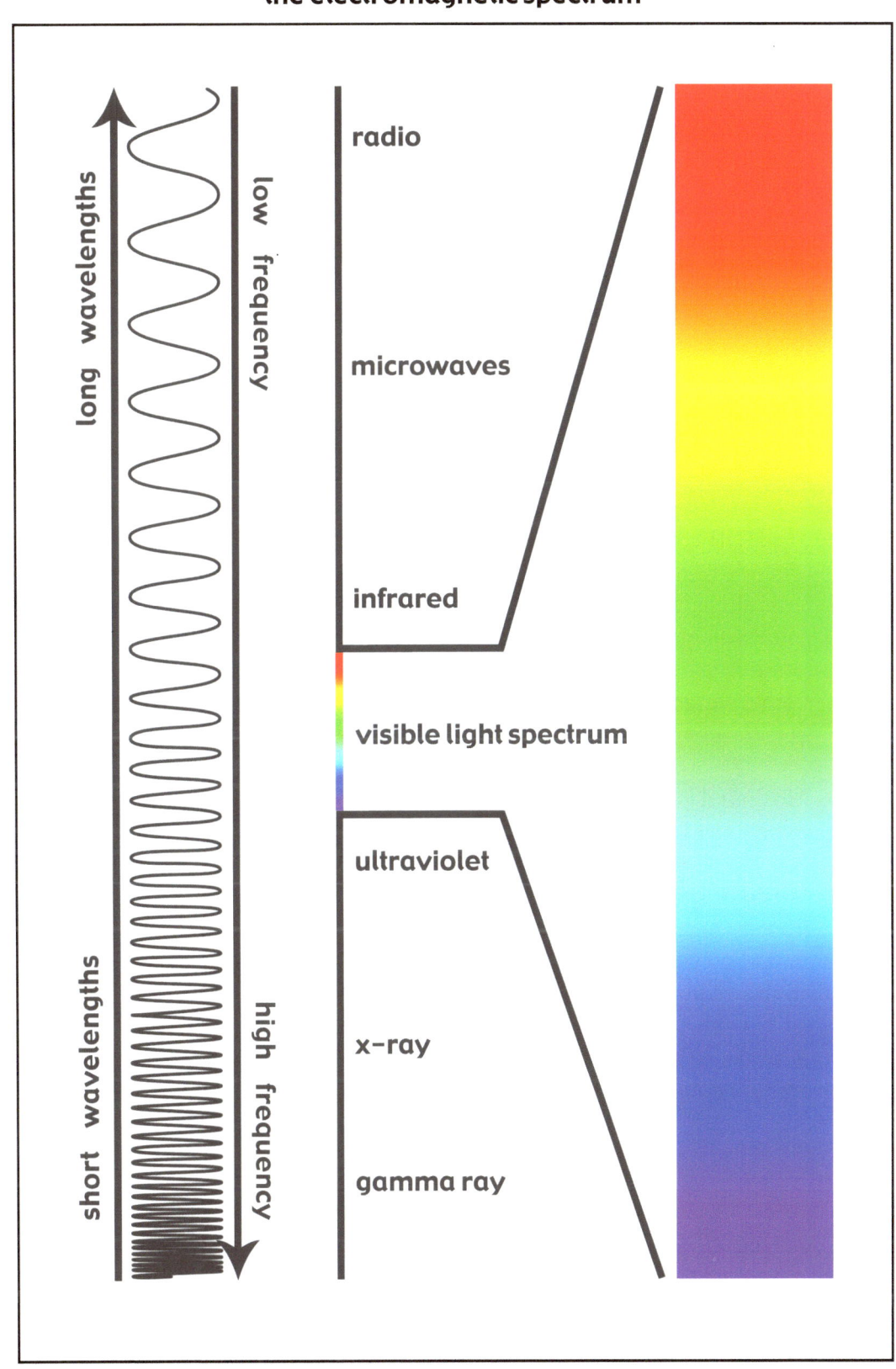

As is further illustrated in the following pages, the color space, also called color gamut, of a computer monitor is smaller and less nuanced than our visible light spectrum. Computer monitors use combinations of red, green, and blue light to display images and text. Most computer monitors these days can display 24-bit color, that is, 8-bits per color channel. There are 3 color channels, red, green, and blue. So there are 8 bits or 256 levels of red, 8 bits or 256 levels of green, and 8 bits or 256 levels of blue. *

This is called the RGB color space and it's based on the Additive Color System. The primary colors of the Additive RGB color model are red, green, and blue. This system applies to media that uses light to describe color, like projectors, computers monitors, and television screens.

The RGB color system is called the additive color system because all the primaries *added* together in equal parts create white. This may seem counterintuitive if your background is in painting or illustration - if you mix red paint with green and blue paint, you definitely do not get white. But monitors display colors using light emitted from a screen, not paint reflected from a surface. And when you add light to light you get something lighter. You can combine the primary colors to create almost any other color.

All digital printers use cyan, magenta, yellow, and black ink to display color. The CMYK color space is based on the Subtractive Color System. The primary colors are cyan, magenta, and yellow. It's called the subtractive color system because all the primaries added together create something close to black. To achieve rich, deep, black shadows, printers always use an additional black ink, denoted by the letter "K." You can combine the primary colors to create almost any other color.

Both the RGB and the CMYK systems share the same color wheel. The primary colors of one are the secondary colors of the other.

* For more about bit depth, see *Chapter 3*.

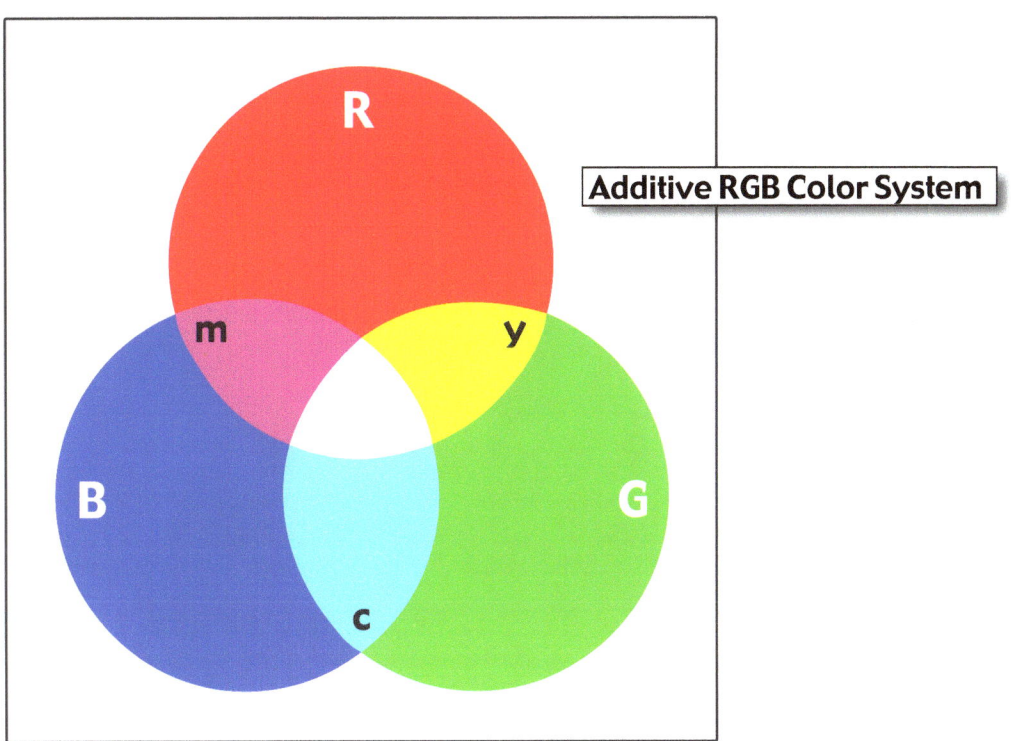

Additive RGB Color System

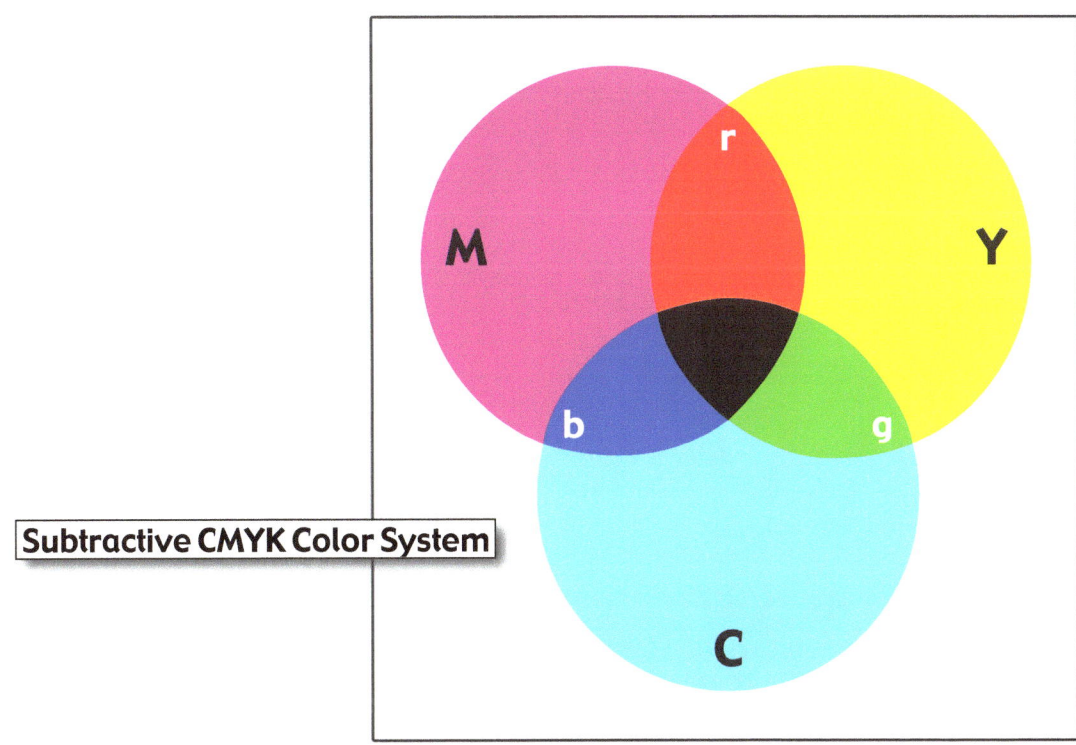

Subtractive CMYK Color System

When you mix all the primaries of either system you get a neutral, white for the additive RGB color system, black for the subtractive CMYK color system. It's a very elegant, practical system.

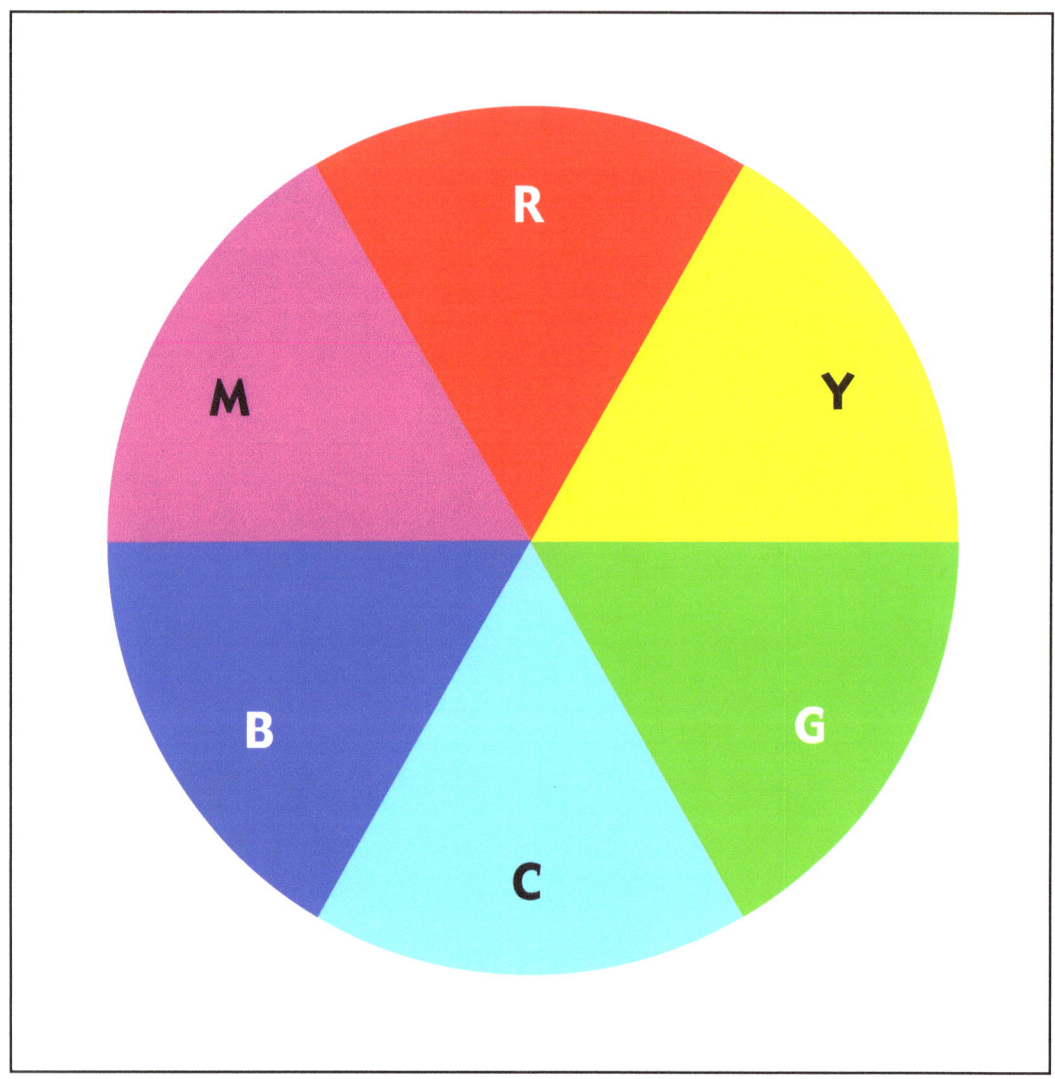

Complementary colors, that is, colors opposite each other on the color wheel, neutralize or balance each other out. When we look at them right next to each other, they seem to vibrate against each other.   This is just one of the many color phenomena artists and scientists continue to explore.

The color wheel is also the basis for the HSB (**H**ue **S**aturation **B**rightness) color system. Every hue has a position on the color wheel, starting with red at 0°, cyan at 180°, and back to red at 360° or 0° – a circle always ends where it starts.   Saturation describes how much of the hue exists in the color, and brightness is pretty much self-explanatory. For example, using the HSB color system, red is defined as H 0° S100% B 100%.

The graph below is a way to visualize color space. The large horseshoe shape represents the visible color spectrum. No medium - this book included - can reproduce the range and nuance of the colors we see, but we can use the graph to compare color gamuts spatially, in terms of size and shape. Notice that it's especially the green and blue areas of the visible light spectrum that are most difficult to reproduce in any medium.

Even though the RGB color gamut is made up of 24-bit color,* which equals16.7 million colors, it doesn't approximate the range and nuance of the colors we can see, or even of film. The triangle shape in the graph below represents a generic RGB gamut. The CMYK color gamut is even smaller. That's not likely to change much as ink technology has been around for a while.

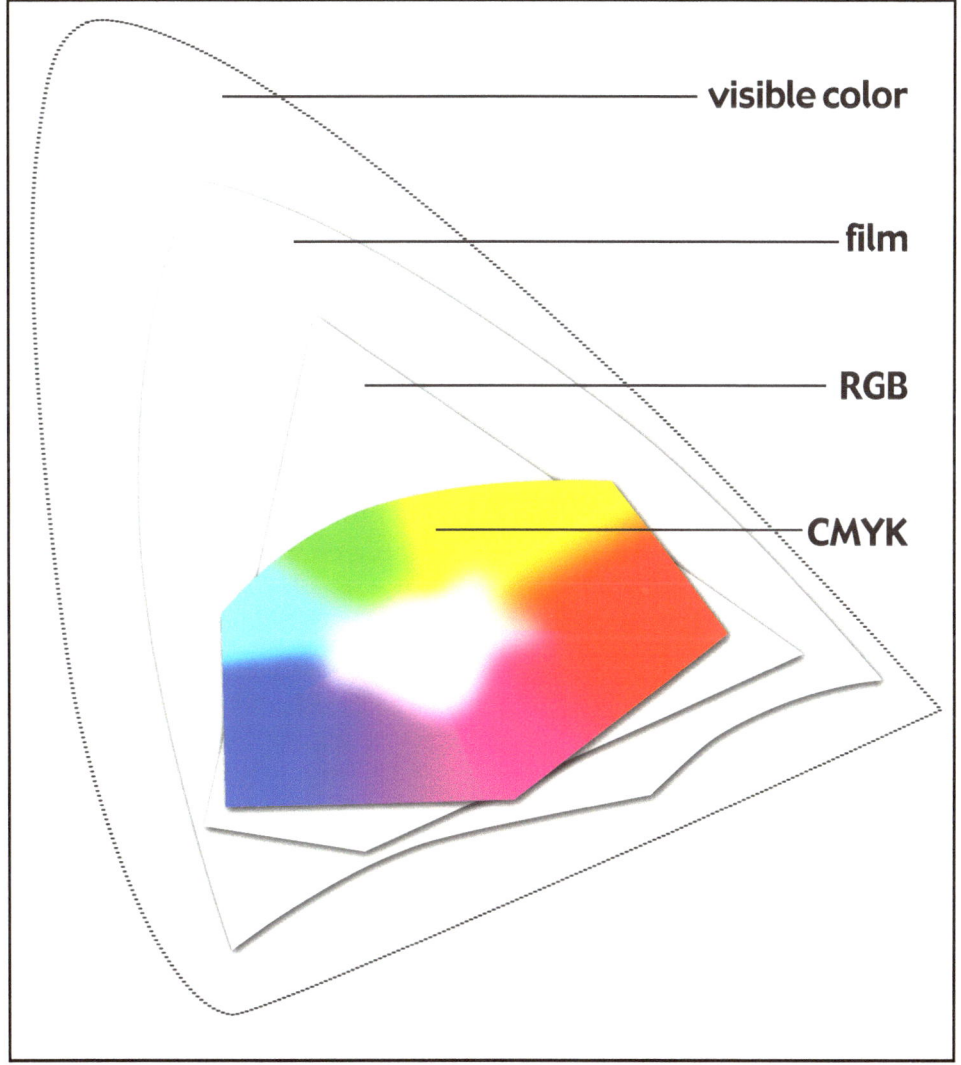

visible color

film

RGB

CMYK

* For more about bit depth, *Chapter 3*.

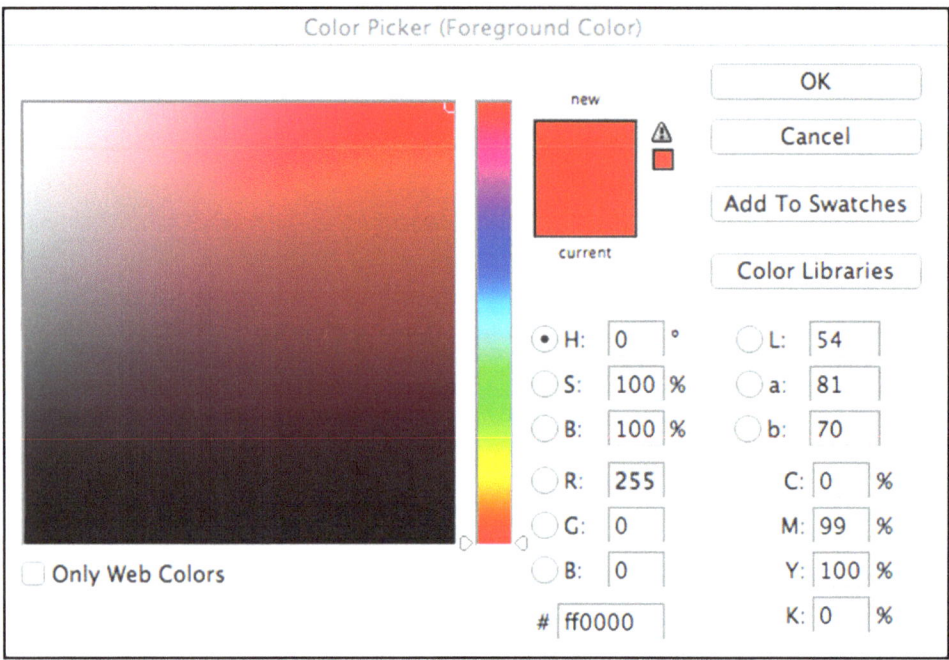

The Photoshop color picker allows you to pick colors using HSB, RGB (256 levels of red, green, and blue from 0 to 255), CMYK, Lab, and web hexadecimal values.

The Lab (**L**ightness, **a** axis of two complementary colors, and **b** axis of two opposing complementary colors) color space is larger than the RGB or the CMYK color space, but it has only a few practical uses because there are no devices that capture or output that much color information.

The web hexadecimal code (for example, ff0000 for red) is used for defining a color in HTML, which is the basic programming code used for web pages. The web color palette is a small color space - only 217 colors. Back in the early days of computer monitors, when they only displayed 256 colors,* Windows machines displayed a different 256 colors than Apple machines, and they only shared 217 colors. Each of the 217 web colors has a 6-character (hexadecimal) HTML code. This is not a big deal anymore as very few people are working with old 256-color monitors.

* For more about bit depth, see *Chapter 3*.

The Photoshop color picker Color Libraries button allow you to pick colors using color matching systems. These are sets of standardized colors, also found in printed swatch books, that allow you to choose a specific color and reproduce it using an offset printing press or in manufacturing using CMYK inks or spot color pigments. The most popular of these are Pantone, Toyo, and Trumatch. Offset printing is more expensive but generally more cost effective for large quantities of prints than other printing methods.

Color Management

A big part of the challenge of working digitally is translating the RGB light emitted from the monitor into the CMYK colors reflected from a print. Monitors display red, green, and blue light, which is slightly different when printed with cyan, magenta, yellow, and black ink on different kinds of paper. Because the RGB color space is larger than the CMYK color space, some colors, especially saturated reds, greens, and blues, don't look the same in print as they do on the screen. These colors are out of gamut. Also, as you may have noticed, the same image can look different on different screens.

You can use RGB, CMYK, Lab, hexadecimal web codes, or color matching systems to make sure a specific color is reproduced accurately throughout the process. They are useful for logos, type or spot colors. But we also want to be able to reproduce colors on all the various devices that we use to capture and display imagery as accurately as possible for continuous tone images such as photographs. This is called color management.

Color Management continued

The International Color Consortium (ICC) has developed a set of standards for generating color profiles that specifically define the color gamut for each device used to capture or display color. Using the same ICC profile on your printer as the one in your file makes it easier to reproduce, or manage, your colors. Fortunately, this is becoming more standardized, and most devices are using the Adobe RGB color profile as the default. If you are printing on your desktop printer, it's likely that your operating system is doing the color management for you. However, if you are printing off-site, you may need to calibrate your monitor so that it gives you an accurate preview of your image in print and change the color profile of the file you give the printer to match theirs. The graph on the following page helps to compare the Adobe RGB and the sRGB ICC profiles.

It's important to remember that it's best not to color manage or change the color profile of your master files; it's only when you're ready for output that you may need to change the color profile of a copy of your master file.*

When preparing images for the screen, make sure you check Embed Color Profile in the Photoshop Save for Web interface, so your colors don't shift.

* For more about workflow, see *Chapter 2*.

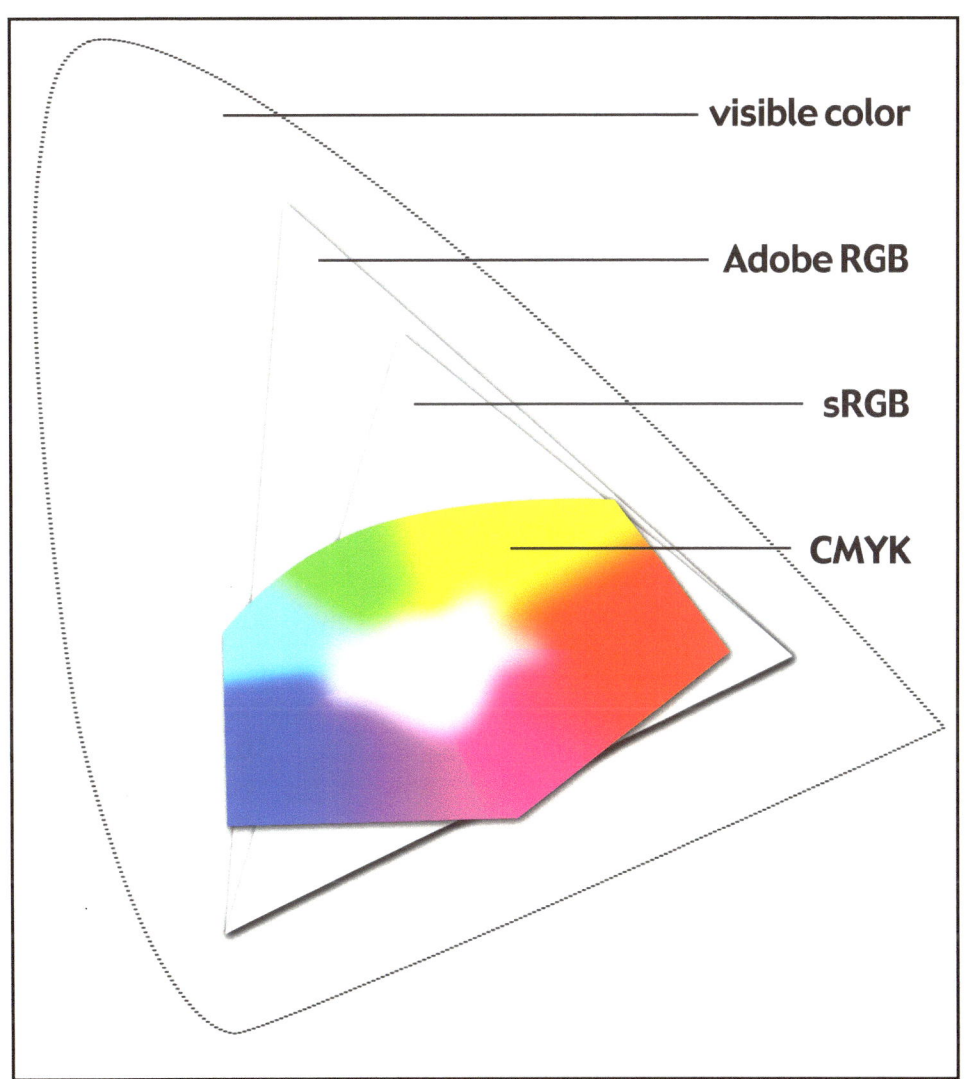

visible color

Adobe RGB

sRGB

CMYK

ABOUT THE AUTHOR

Artist and educator, Isabella La Rocca received her B.A. in Fine Arts from the University of Pennsylvania and her M.F.A. in Photography from Indiana University. She began her teaching career in 1991 while in graduate school. Since then she has taught thousands of students photography and digital media, from introductory courses to advanced seminars, in state universities, private colleges, art schools, and community colleges. She has witnessed and participated in the evolution of photography from analog to digital and her students have included digital immigrants and digital natives. "I love to connect with people when they learn. I live for the moment the light goes on in my student's mind. I've developed a holistic method that integrates essential theory with training and practice. Throughout my teaching career, I've reviewed hundreds of text books, training discs, and e-learning sites; my intention for Pixnexus has been to develop the handbook of my dreams, that I've yet to encounter anywhere else."

www.ingramcontent.com/pod-product-compliance
Lightning Source LLC
Chambersburg PA
CBHW051100180526
45172CB00002B/713